HEALING RAIN

My Journey Experiencing Healing through Worship

by Diana Scates

© Copyright 2018 – Diana Scates
All rights reserved. This book is protected by the copyrights laws of the United States of America. This book may not be copied or reprinted for commercial gain or profit. No part of this publication may be reproduced, stored in a retrieval system or transmitted in any form or bay any means; for example, electronic, photocopy, or recording without prior written permission from the author. The only exception is brief quotations printed in reviews as well as occasional page copying for personal or group study. Permission will be granted upon request. Some names were changed to maintain the privacy of the people involved.

All Scripture quotations, unless otherwise noted, are taken from the New King James Version (NKJV), Copyright © 1982 by Thomas Nelson, Inc.

Other versions used are:
NIV – Scriptures are taken from the Holy Bible: New International Version, Copyright © 1973, 1978. 1984 by the International Bible Society.
KJV – Scripture are taken from The King James Study Bible, Copyright © 2011 by Thomas Nelson, Inc.
AMP - Scripture are taken from The Amplified Bible, Copyright © 1987 by The Zondervan Corporation.
NLT - Scripture are taken from New Living Translation, Copyright © 1996, 2004, 2015 by Tyndale House Foundation.

Cover design by Diana Scates of Rivers of Judah Ministries
www.riversofjudah.com
Photos by Lance Scates - lance@riversofjudah.com and Joe Leineweber from Pexels.
Collaborators: Lance Scates, Paul Cuny, and Charles Portela

Edited by: 5 Fold Media® LLC
5701 East Circle Dr. #338, Cicero, NY 13039
Phone: 315.570.3333, Ext. 3 | Fax: 888.289.5755
5foldmedia.com
And Jeffrey Pelton
http://jeffreypelton.com
http://inscribeministries.com

Printed in the United States of America by CreateSpace
First Printing 2018
To Order Contact:: diana@riverofjudah.com

ISBN-13: 978-1-7324390-0-9

I dedicate this work to God. Without His love and mercy, I would not be alive today to publish this book. I consider this opportunity to write this memoir to be part of my destiny.

To our friends and the ones we knew and prayed with who battled this terrible disease called cancer. Some of them are still with us running the race, and others have gone to be with the Father.

My love goes to my dear friends Rita Pires' (Ritinha), Luci Almeida, and Juvenal Auge's family. You were heroes. You fought a big battle like mighty warriors and we had the privilege to be alongside you in prayers and encouragement. Now you are with the Father in eternity, but your legacy remains.

ENDORSEMENTS

Healing Rain is a touching portrayal of the journey through a life-threatening crisis of cancer - a crisis that is all too familiar these days. Diana Scates is a strong woman of God who speaks openly about her journey that includes the shock of the discovery, denial, and her desperation for a touch from God. *Healing Rain* is more than a book about one person's journey through a crisis. Diana shares highly valuable insights with practical applications that were gained from her time in the fire of life. Her insights to overcoming can be adopted by anyone on this journey. *Healing Rain* is a book about a woman hearing God's voice in a desperate time and deciding to literally stake her life on God's words. *Healing Rain* is a book about her journey, but it is also a book about a loving God who would not leave her during very dark times. I have been deeply moved by *Healing Rain* and I give it my strongest recommendation!

Paul L. Cuny
President, MarketPlace Leadership International
www.marketplaceleadership.com
Author of Secrets of the Kingdom Economy & Nehemiah People

As Diana's husband, I was also surprised by the doctor's final words that my wife was diagnosed with cancer. So, in agreement early on, we started to make wise decisions, such as to filter out any negative words from us or from others. We also never accepted the cancer as ours, for it was an illegal disease in her body. This book is about an amazing wife who never gave up, but worshipped Jesus with her flute even in the midst of pain. She could be physically weak, but her spirit was strong in Him to come out victorious, glorifying the Father. I will never forget those days embraced by God's love as He sung over and strengthened us. There are not words enough to thank the Lord and to all of those who blessed us so much. To Him be all the glory, honor and praise.

Lance Scates – Husband, Worshiper, and Caregiver
Co-founder of Rivers of Judah Ministries
www.riversofjudah.com

Healing Rain is a testimony of an overcomer who has used her faith as powerful support to defeat all adversities, both physical and emotional, and to develop an exemplary spiritual intelligence. As eyewitnesses, co-protagonists, friends, and brethren in Christ of this victorious journey, we can say that today you have in hand a book from an author who has a profound experience and resilience that will motivate you to overcome any challenge that you can possibly face.

Anthony & Fernanda Portigliatti PhD
President, Chancellor and Pastors of
Florida Christian University
Orlando, Florida - www.fcuonline.com

Diana has walked through the fire of facing cancer and by God's grace she came out victorious. In this book, she is open and candid about the battles she faced as she approached cancer. As you read, you can learn on how to be an overcomer and experience the many victories she went through. Cancer is so prevalent today that many simply become paralyzed with fear when the word is mentioned. However, through this book, you will find a living testimony of someone who—with the help of God, family, friends, doctors, and many praying for her—has learned to overcome fear and guide many others through what she walked through. This is for anyone fighting cancer, for those who are taking care of loved ones with cancer, or for those who would like to know on how to be better prepared on helping others.

Bradley Stuart
Director at Yada International
http://yadainternational.com

I've known Diana Scates for a long time and we have been good friends. This book will become paramount to the lives of those who believe that faith can actually move all things. As you read it, you will feel inspired to believe more in God, to know that He is immutable, and that He keeps His promises. Above all, the reader will see that God always has the last word. We cannot explain all the purposes and paths that God draws in life, but we know that He has the final say. Believe! And see in the pages of this book words that make your faith grow.

Mercia Leite Sousa
Realtor, Orlando, Florida
http://vizinhodomickey.com

It is not difficult to speak about Diana Scates in a nutshell. The challenge lies in what she went through a few years ago when she faced death for many days. However, she knew how to trust and wait for God's intervention. Jesus came at the right time to rescue her history as a woman, wife, and Christian servant. Her experience of surviving deadly cancer led her to experience God's undeserving favor and to relate with compassion as well as empathy towards others who face the same reality as she did. In this book, Diana shares nothing more than her authentic story to help others to believe that it is possible to cross over "through the valley of the shadow of death" and arrive in the other side safe of abundant provision that life brings. Good reading!

Gilmar Sousa
Pastor and Hospital Chaplain, Orlando, Florida

ACKNOWLEDGEMENTS

I would like to acknowledge very important people who made this book possible.

Thank you to my husband, Lance. For your love and support from the first day when I was diagnosed with cancer until the end. You have left me without words to express my gratitude. Your encouragement and your devotion to God lifted me up during some difficult days of my life. I love you so much.

Thank you to my close family: Geraldo, Selma, Rosanna, Rubens, Ruben, Jessica, Núria, and Edna. You chose to enter wholeheartedly into this battle against this horrible disease, so unknown to us all, without hesitation and fear. Your prayers and emotional support were very important for my recovery.

Thank you to my cousins Lucia and Alex (and families). You cheered for us all the time.

Thank you to all Scates' family and all prayer warriors who stood with us in the gap.

Thank you to my dear friends: Anthony and Fernanda Portigliatti. You both embraced this journey with us in many details. You rock! I cannot thank you enough.

Thank you to Mercia and Gilmar Sousa, Betinho and Marcia Boselli, Raimundo, Marcia and all Veloso's family, Valeria and Eduardo Oliveira, and Boletti's family who encouraged and prayed for us. Thank you from the bottom of my heart!

Thank you to my friends Andrea Almeida, Dani Veloso, and Valéria Cristina Oliveira who were present and willing to talk and laugh, making me feel that life was normal again.

Thank you to Oneida and family who interceded for us tirelessly.

Thank you to Luzia, Sonia, and Mercia who helped me organize my house when I couldn't.

Thank you to all the dear pastors in Orlando who prayed and encouraged us during this journey.

Thank you to all the doctors and nurses who helped me go through this challenging period of treatment.

To all my deepest gratitude!

"Your word is a lamp to my feet and a light to my path."

Psalm 119:105

TABLE OF CONTENTS

Foreword 11
Introduction 13

Part 1 – *My Journey*
Chapter 1 - The Provision to My Journey 17
Chapter 2 - God is in Control of Everything
　　　　　　All the Time 25
Chapter 3 - The Results 33

Part 2 – *The Healing Rain*
Chapter 4 - Healing Rain 43

Part 3 – *The Preparation*
Chapter 5 - The Second Consequence of
　　　　　　the Divine Encounter 47
Chapter 6 - The Support Team Arrives! 53
Chapter 7 - Second Chemo 57

Part 4 – *Nuggets of Truth*
Chapter 8 -   Dove's Eyes 63
Chapter 9 -   Cheerful Heart 69
Chapter 10 - Don't Possess Diseases 75
Chapter 11 - Dealing with Fear 79
Chapter 12 - Resting Place without Striving 85
Chapter 13 - The Blood That Heals 95

Part 5 – *The End of the Journey*
Chapter 14 - The End of Chemotherapy 103
Chapter 15 - The Last Part of the Treatment – Mercy........... 107
Chapter 16 - Final Message 111
Prayer for Healing 113
Appendix 115

Hope

FOREWORD

I suppose there is nothing more feared in our modern culture than a diagnosis of cancer! One would be hard-pressed to find even a single family that had not suffered the terrible and painful loss of a friend or loved one due to that ruthless disease. Millions of wonderful people, and thousands of children die each year from its cruel grasp. The very mention of the disease implies a sentence of suffering and death!

However, once in a while we cross paths with someone who faced cancer, defeated it, overcame it, and lived to tell about it. Such is the amazing experience of my friend Diana Scates.

Diana is a lovely young professional woman who, in the prime of her life, was diagnosed with cancer. As you might expect the initial impact was devastating! However, she rose up to accept the challenge. It's important to understand Diana accepted the challenge; she never accepted the cancer!

If you have the pleasure of meeting her, Diana would not impress you as a particularly "strong" woman. She's tall and slender in a delicate sort of way, very soft spoken, and polite. But beneath that soft feminine exterior lies a warrior's heart. She desperately wanted to live and was willing to face the greatest battle of her life and do whatever was necessary to make that happen.

This book is the record of Diana's journey of decision, determination, discipline, sacrifice, and most of all her faith. Diana wants her story told as a testimony of hope to all who may be facing cancer or any other life-threatening disease. She honestly believes because she fought and won you can fight and win.

Missionary Dan Duke
A Call to the Nations Ministry
www.fireandglory.com

"For I know the thoughts that I think toward you, says the Lord, throughts of peace and not of evil, to give you a future and a hope."
Jeremiah 29:11

INTRODUCTION

God has a special way of turning a dreadful event in our lives into something that inspires, encourages, or opens one's ears (and heart) to listen to Him. His love towards us is so indescribable that the lack of words leaves us with only one option in receiving this great love: believe and receive His love by faith. The purpose of this memoir is to connect and revive memories of God's unmeasurable love, His sweet goodness, and His deepest truth in faith for His glory.

I love to read biographies and watch movies inspired on true stories. Personal stories are indisputable because of their uniqueness. The Bible is full of stories from people from different backgrounds, races, and ethnicities who have inspired many. A few months after I finished my last radiation treatment, I felt the desire to compile my journey. Though I like to journal, I knew this particular experience must be shared with a larger audience. I confess that I was caught by surprise with this thought, but I accepted the challenge.

The pages that are ahead of you will take you through my personal journey of the darkest season of my life as of today. During that season of life, I had the privilege of counting on my family and friends who gave me all the support I needed, for which I am most grateful. However, they were the supporting team and I was the protagonist of this story. As a protagonist, I had to walk that challenging path by myself, wiring my thoughts and aligning my faith to focus on my cure. Everyone has a different story, but two things we all have in common: our ability to decide to be resilient walking through difficult paths of life; and our desire to let God be a part (or not be a part) of this journey. My advice to you is to run fearlessly to God instead of running away from Him, so you can embrace His affection towards you. He definitely will cover you with His goodness.

I hope my personal journey unlocks your heart to receive a fresh insight (revelation) of His love towards you despite the circumstances of life we all face daily. Enjoy your reading!

Diana Scates
Co-founder of Rivers of Judah Ministries - www.riversofjudah.com

"Though I walk through the valley of the shadow of death, I will fear no evil; for You are with me."

Psalm 23:4

Part 1
My Journey

The Provision for
My Journey

THE PROVISION FOR MY JOURNEY

"Life is like a box of chocolates. You never know what you are going to get." —Forrest Gump

Journey is the act of traveling from one place to another. It is a passage, peregrination, expedition.[1] We don't dwell in it.

I had just returned from the gym after a long day of work and decided to stretch in front of a mirror. When I was slowly pulling my shoulders up and down, I noticed a bump forming on one side. I tried the movement again and the results were the same. *"What an odd thing!"* I thought.

It is always good to call for a second pair of eyes, so I asked my husband to check what I was doing and tell me what he was seeing. He confirmed what I saw. My doctor's appointment was close and we decided to mention it to her.

It was the end of November and we had already started our preparation for our trip to Brazil to spend Christmas and New Year's with our families. Our expectation for this gathering was high, because we hadn't had an opportunity to be there for the last two years.

Truly, we didn't know what was ahead of us, but God always has the provision already prepared for any situation when we obey.

Then the word of the Lord came to him, saying, "Get away from here and turn eastward, and hide by the Brook Cherith, which flows into the Jordan. And it will be that you shall drink from the brook, and I have commanded the ravens to feed you there" (1 Kings 17:2-4).

At this point, not knowing what lay ahead of me, I decided to believe in God's provision for this situation as Elijah did.

When my already scheduled appointment came, she looked at the bump on my shoulder and left the room to speak with another doctor. I thought this was strange, but I let it go. She recommended some tests. I told her we had plans to travel in a few weeks, so she expedited everything.

God was taking care of me one more time. In a week, I could return to the doctor for the results.

When I returned, Dr. N. called Dr. M, head of the clinic, to speak with me. I have never had two doctors in the same room explaining something to me before, so it was somewhat different. I knew something unusual was going on.

He asked me some questions about my symptoms, my plans for Christmas, and said that he needed a biopsy of that area in order to have a more precise diagnosis. Even though he was very calm and careful with his words, it was not very clear to me what was going on. After some talking, I asked him, "What exactly do you think it is?"

He said that it could be an infection or lymphoma. I had heard about lymphoma before, but at that time I was not familiar with the symptoms of the disease. I asked for an explanation. After a pause, he told me this was a treatable illness and that I should not be worried about it at that point. He told me to enjoy my time with my family. However, he mentioned the most important thing to do was to schedule the biopsy as soon as I arrived home from our Christmas vacation. I turned again to him and asked, "Is this some type of cancer? I don't have any history of this disease in my family." He never used the word *cancer* at any time, but he told me that lymphoma was treatable and I needed to spend time with my family as much as I could.

I was very thankful that my doctor did not speak negatively about the case or scare me. On the contrary, he was wise enough to say everything he needed to say at that moment without needlessly upsetting me with an inconclusive diagnosis.

This was part of God's provision for my journey, even though I did not realize it at the time. According to the Merriam-Webster Dictionary, provision is *"the fact or state of being prepared beforehand; and a measure taken beforehand to deal with a need or contingency."*[2]

In this case, God was providing the right doctors with the right attitude that I could handle. I was being prepared to walk in a new season of my life unfolding ahead.

THE PREPARATION FOR THE TRIP

I left the clinic, feeling very uncertain about the future. I called my husband and explained all the possibilities and my thoughts. He reassured me that I should not worry about the diagnosis until we had the results of the biopsy. I had no history of cancer in my family, so the possibility was low anyway. At the same time, Lance encouraged me to lift my spirit up.

As I drove home, I prayed and felt a peace I could not explain. Such peace comforted me every day. Only God can give the kind of peace that I was feeling. It is the absolute assurance that you are not alone and that He is holding your hand, embracing and carrying you. It is priceless.

In my prayers, I gave thanks to God for His sovereignty over every situation and for every person He was going to use to help me through the process. I knew He was in control of everything. I surrendered the situation, my life, and my thoughts to Him. I asked for grace and wisdom to guide us through whatever we needed to do. I asked God to increase my hope and my faith to always believe in Him. I decided to trust God, focusing on the present moment and not allowing worry to rob me of my strength. I did not believe that the biopsy would indicate a serious diagnosis anyway, as I felt fine.

The way that we focus and believe is very important. Many times in the Psalms, David wrote about his frustrations and failures, but he always ended by turning his praises to God and declaring Him sovereign over all.

Be merciful to me, O God, for man would swallow me up; fighting all day he oppresses me. My enemies would hound me all day, for there are many who fight against me, O Most High. Whenever I am afraid, I will trust in You. In God (I will praise His word), in God I have put my trust; I will not fear. What can flesh do to me? All day they twist my words; all their thoughts are against me for evil. They gather together, they hide, they mark my steps, when they lie in wait for my life. Shall they escape by iniquity? In anger cast down the peoples, O God! You number my wanderings; put my tears into Your bottle; are they not in Your book? When I cry out to You, then my enemies will turn back; this I know, because God is for me. In God (I will praise His word), in the Lord (I will praise His word), in God I have put my trust; I will not be afraid. What can man do to me? Vows made to You are binding upon me, O God; I will render praises to You, for You have delivered my soul from death. Have You not kept my feet from falling, that I may walk before God in the light of the living? (Psalm 56)

Deliver me from my enemies, O my God; defend me from those who rise up against me. Deliver me from the workers of iniquity, and save me from bloodthirsty men. (Psalm 59:1-2).

But I will sing of Your power; yes, I will sing aloud of Your mercy in the morning; for You have been my defense and refuge in the day of my trouble. To You, O my Strength, I will sing praises; for God is my defense, my God of mercy. (Psalm 59:16-17).

This is an exercise we need to practice with our soul. Otherwise, our emotions will collapse and we will allow our circumstances to rule over us, preventing our faith from growing.

The rest of the year was very hectic for us. We had many challenges and many victories. We finished the purchase of our first home in the United States and we were very happy about that. We couldn't wait for our vacation time with the family, but at the same time we were not aware of what the future held. In addition, our agenda would not permit us to deal with infirmity. The ministry schedule for that year was planned already and many promises were coming to pass. I had just started my master's degree and my husband had already finished his B.A. Our dreams were beginning to come true. During that week, we put everything aside and flew to Brazil.

THE TRIP

My sister warmly received us in São Paulo. We ministered in worship at their church during that weekend and it was a blessing. On Monday, we traveled again to the city where our parents lived. This was the best time of the year to see friends and family at once, because they all came together to one city. It was the reason that we had high expectations. Our goal was to rest and spend time with family and friends. I didn't have plans to have doctor visits or anything of that nature; I just wanted to rest.

Christmas came and when all the activities returned to normal, I decided to speak to my parents about what I had discovered before I came to see them. I began by saying that everything was fine and we didn't have any reason for concern. (I really didn't want to spend my vacation visiting doctors and doing tests. In the past, we had used our vacation time to visit doctors, but this time we just wanted to enjoy family.)

It weeks did not happen the way we had planned. After hearing my report, my family convinced me to visit some specialists to get a second opinion. One of the doctors suggested doing an invasive procedure to collect material for a test. I hoped for an immediate diagnosis. It was very painful and the result was the same as Dr. M's—you need a biopsy.

One of the doctors told me he thought it was a lymphoma and that I needed to be prepared for treatment. I didn't like what I heard. It bothered me the way he spoke to me. It is so important to know how to communicate with people, especially in the medical field. Moreover, my parents heard it too; I didn't like that either. I left the clinic, thinking the doctor jumped the gun. I told my parents that we didn't need to be concerned because we didn't have any history of cancer in our family and that God was in control of everything. We got in the car and prayed for peace. (A few months later, we found out that this doctor was right, but for now, we were back to square one.) For the rest of our vacation, we agreed we would enjoy every moment with family and friends. There would be no more doctors or exams. As planned, the next stop was to visit family in Rio de Janeiro and come back home.

FINALLY, VACATION

During the few days that we were in Rio visiting family, we really felt that we were on vacation. Our flight back to the US was supposed to leave Saturday, so Friday morning on our way to the beach, my husband decided to stop at the travel agency to confirm the tickets. To our surprise, our flight was canceled and they were suggesting we leave that same day. I could not do that because we still had things to do there, in addition to all the arrangements that we had with the family until Saturday. After phone calls and airport visits, we were able to move the flight to Sunday morning instead.

ENDNOTES:

1. Journey. In *Dictionary.com*. Retrieved on April 28, 2017, from
   http://www.dictionary.com/browse/journey

2. Provision. In *Merriam-Webster.com*. Retrieved on April 28, 2017, from https://www.merriam-webster.com/dictionary/provision

Two

GOD IS IN CONTROL OF EVERYTHING ALL THE TIME

"He shall cover you with His feathers, and under His wings you shall take refuge; His truth shall be your shield and buckler"
(Psalms 91:4)

There is no doubt that God is in control of everything at all times as we trust in Him. From the beginning of this journey we were aware that something out of the ordinary was happening, beginning with the flight cancellation as well as all the rest. We had an overwhelming sense of rest, confidence, and expectation as we knew that the Lord was orchestrating this whole situation with a specific purpose that we would only understand in the future.

Sunday came and it was time to go back home. We arrived at the airport, and it was time to go through security and give that final, emotional Brazilian goodbye to our family before we passed through the first gate. This was not easy. Everyone was on board the plane when the pilot's voice came on the speaker, saying they were having technical difficulties. Finally, after one hour without air conditioning inside the plane with all the seats taken in the height of summer, we left for Miami, Florida to make our connection.

A divine encounter was unfurling in front of our eyes, but at this point we had not noticed. We arrived in Miami at the end of the day. Being the first week of the year, the airport was chaotic. We couldn't find a baggage cart and because our flight had been delayed one hour we could not make our connection to Orlando. Finally, we arrived at the airline counter where they informed us that because we were late, the only available flight would be the next day, Monday. This was not an option for us, so we had to go to the counter of the Brazilian airline whose flight had been delayed and see what they could do for us. We were supposed to arrive on Saturday, and now there we were stuck in Miami on Sunday afternoon. We couldn't miss work on Monday. But God had prepared all these situations with a specific purpose.

DIVINE ENCOUNTER

We went to the counter of the Brazilian airline to speak with the manager and see what he could do. We were praying for a solution. When we arrived there, we noticed that we were not the only ones in the same difficulty due to the delay in Rio. The airline company decided to put us on another flight that same night to Orlando. Thanks to God we were able to get home that same day.

While we were waiting for them to print the new boarding passes and finalize the transaction, a young couple with a child arrived and took their place in line behind us. As I chatted with the woman about all the delays, I realized that they were scheduled for the same flight that was canceled on

Saturday too. They had also been on the same flight to Miami. They were there because they had lost their connection to Rochester. *What a coincidence,* I thought. During my short conversation with her, we decided to exchange business cards, thinking only about suing the airline for all the inconvenience they had caused us.

I looked at her card, not paying attention to her workplace but only to her name, which was quite unusual—Dr. T. When I finished asking how to pronounce her name, my husband announced that our new tickets were ready and we needed to run to the gate. He spoke a little bit with her husband too and we left this friendly couple, hoping they would also find a way to get home on that same day.

This was a divine encounter. The flight cancellation had put us in a position to meet this couple for those few minutes in order to exchange some personal information. It was all part of God's plan. At that moment, we knew that God was orchestrating this whole situation. We had a feeling inside of us that something was taking place, but we could not explain what that was exactly. When we realized that we lost our connection to Orlando, we thought, *"God is behind this. Let's keep our eyes open."*

We left the airline counter with our ticket in hand and we were looking for the gate that we were supposed to board. During our fast pace toward the gate, I looked at her card again: "Mayo Clinic, Dr. T. M. Radiology Department." When I read that, I froze in the middle of the craziness of the airport lobby. I felt something in my stomach. My husband didn't notice what had happened until he realized that I was not walking with him anymore. I was in shock. He came back to me and asked what had happened. I showed him the card and he asked, "Why are you concerned?"

I said, "Don't you think this has something to do with the biopsy that I need to do in the next few weeks? I think this encounter was not in vain and God has a plan for this." At that moment, I knew I would need her contact information in the future and the results of the biopsy would be related.

After that, I was quiet and my head was full of questions to God. I felt uncertain about my future. We were lost in what appeared as meaningless obstructions to our plans, but God was about to give us a divine appointment that would change our lives. My husband started to encourage me to put every concern in God's hand and wait for the biopsy's result. I held on to the card from this divine appointment. It was a long day for us.

COMING HOME AND THE BEGINNING OF NEW CHALLENGES

Ah! It was very good to be home safe and sound. That same week we returned to our normal activities. At the church, the winter conference had just begun and that same week on Friday; we restarted our prayer meetings at Rivers of Judah Ministries (our house of prayer ministry).

My next visit to the doctor was scheduled at the end of January. Prior to that appointment, I began to notice some "allergies" on my skin. They were the consequence of my diagnosis, but I didn't know it at the time. Finally, my visit with the surgeon arrived. He and his staff were very attentive before my surgery. Everything was new to me. Dr. P. explained all the steps and procedures to us. I tried to hear his opinion about the possible diagnoses, but he preferred to wait for the results of the surgery. It was a very good conversation, and we left there not knowing what to expect but trusting God was in control. This entire situation was new for us, so it was a challenge. There was no turning back, as we had only one way to go. It was straight ahead, surrendering every day to God's care.

Very early in the morning on February 3rd, I checked in for the procedure. I have never had surgery before and my family and close friends were far away. My loving husband took good care of me, encouraging me to look at the Father's eyes all the time in order not to lose sight of trust and hope. I felt very uncomfortable in this situation. It seemed like a dream and one in which I should run away. I felt a mixture between fearing the unknown and maintaining my faith. It was a battle. God the Father saw my predicament and expressed His care and love for me.

Like David, many times my mind fought with my emotions, declaring that the Father will do everything to make me feel peace in the middle of my situation. This was just a biopsy, yet my soul and my emotions were going wild. I had to command my soul to be quiet and trust in God many times.

Return to your rest, my soul, for the Lord has been good to you (Psalms 116:7 NIV).

God was so good that even when my mind and heart were experiencing this turmoil, I knew there were a lot of people praying for me. God filled my heart with supernatural peace in my prayers before Him. My husband was beside me, always encouraging me and reminding me that everything was going to be all right. I knew it was hard for him too, seeing the one he loved going through moments like this. In addition, God chose lovely nurses to take care of me at that particular moment.

Once in surgery room, it was God, the doctors, and me. To my surprise, there was a gesture of love from the Father, as a nurse with a large smile approached me, introducing herself: "Hi, my name is Oneida. I will prepare you for the surgery." My heart was at peace as Oneida was the name of one of our faithful intercessors. It is not a common name, especially in US, so I saw it as a lovely gesture from God, saying, *"Daughter, I am taking care of you, even on the details. Don't forget about this."* It was a clear sign of the divine for me. That gesture of God's love helped my feeling regarding the surgery, granting me peace from that moment on. My confidence in God's love for me was so strong that there was no room for fear.

On the way into surgery, the anesthesia kicked in and I fell asleep. When I woke up, I was in the recovery room. Dr. P. came to speak with me. He said that we should wait for the biopsy in order to get the results. However, at that moment I had a strong feeling about the results. The nurses could not hide their sadness and concern and said, "Good luck." One more time, I surrendered that moment to God's hand because there was nothing I could do. I could only wait and trust in Him. A couple of hours later I was at home and resting.

For a person who had a healthy lifestyle and never had to be concerned about sickness and things of this nature, this was very difficult. There were many things we did not know but had to learn quickly—stay at home to recover, sleep more, and take medication. These were unusual experiences for me and very challenging, but God uses challenging situations to expand our trust and faith in Him. I could not do much, but I welcomed the difficult situations knowing that God would be glorified somehow in all of it. We were confident He would carry us on this journey. Actually, a new season of our life was unfolding from that moment on.

My brethren, count it all joy when you fall into various trials, knowing that the testing of your faith produces patience (James 1:2-3).

The Result

Three

THE RESULT

Every new season comes with new challenges and new battles to overcome. In the days ahead, I was recovering from the surgery and waiting for Dr. P.'s phone call with my results. During this time, I received many visitors. Among them was a dear friend with whom I shared my experience at the Miami airport and the business card that I exchanged with the woman I met there. I showed her the card and asked her opinion, wondering if I should contact her with some of my questions. She held the card and read it, surprised. She turned to me and asked, "Diana, do you know what the Mayo Clinic is?"

I said, "No, a medical school?" She explained that it was the largest medical clinic research center in the US. She highly encouraged me to send her an e-mail. On her advice I was encouraged to write an e-mail to the woman I met at the airport.

My husband and I were praying constantly. Even in the midst of uncertainty, full of questions, we felt a supernatural inner peace that we couldn't explain. Many times, we preferred not to speak about the subject because we didn't want to raise possibilities or anticipate thoughts that would threaten our peace. There wasn't much we could do at this point except wait for the results to arrive. We were just trying to live our lives as normally as possible.

Finally, on the night of February 9th I received a call from Dr. P. with my diagnosis. He confirmed that I was diagnosed with Hodgkin's lymphoma. I felt the shock of the news in my stomach. Probably the tone of my voice changed, even thought I was trying to act normal and confident. I had learned from my childhood that whatever happens in life, I should face it with my head up, seeking a solution for every problem. At that moment, I had few questions to him. I basically wanted to know what the next step would be in order to move on throughout this journey. I hung up the phone and called a friend of ours with whom we were meeting that evening - Tony Portigliatti. He was still on his way home and was shocked with the news. I asked him to keep us in his prayers at that moment, as we were calling our families after I finished talking with him. He encouraged us to stay still in the Lord and trust in Him.

We called a dear missionary couple friend of ours, Dan and Marti Duke, to share the news. They prayed peace over us and encouraged us to keep our eyes on Him in all that lay ahead. Even though it was late at night in Brazil, I felt that I needed to call my parents right away. They were already waiting for my call and put me on speakerphone. I went directly to the point and told them that the diagnosis of the biopsy was Hodgkin's lymphoma. I also mentioned that God was in control of everything and that we didn't accept this situation, so we were determined to believe in what the Word of God said; that was our motto, so we could get through this. I told them it would be very important to me for them to believe with us and turn their eyes to the sovereignty of God who was more than able to operate in miracles, signs, and wonders. God would provide strength and supply everything that we needed. They said they would support us and agreed. We talked a little bit more and hung up. Nobody cried or felt desperate.

At that moment, we felt that we needed to set up a plan of action and were secure that God would show us what to do and where to go. From that moment on, we started to share with our close family the way that we decided to walk by faith. It was very important to us that we remained united by faith in Christ and focused so we could see the supernatural plan of God.

One day after receiving the results of the biopsy, I sent an e-mail to the doctor we met at the airport. It was clear now that this was a divine appointment. I described what I was going through, some questions I had, an oncologist's referral in the Orlando area, and asked if she recommended having a second opinion on the pathological exam, especially as I didn't have any history of this disease in my family.

She responded quickly, asking for my cell phone number as she would prefer to speak with me by phone. Happy and thankful to hear from her, I answered her immediately.

On that same day, February 11th, my husband picked me up at work in order to take me to Dr. P. for a post-surgery visit. When he parked at the clinic, my phone rang. It was the doctor whom God put in our lives through a divine appointment. I told her the whole situation, and she answered all my questions. She suggested that I could send my pathological material to her in order to run a second opinion on it. Even though she was very clearly saying that the error margin on this situation is low, she would do that to give me peace of mind. She also recommended two hospitals in my area that I could visit. These recommendations opened doors for us in finding an oncologist who could help us with the treatment. All of this happened during a one-week period. It was a very intense moment in our lives and this was just the beginning.

AN OASIS AHEAD OF US

During that week, a dear friend, David Quinlan, who is musician, was in town. We decided to meet with him to worship the Father God together. It was a great blessing for us as we felt comforted by the Father. Cliff and Liz were there as well; we felt blessed to have friends like them. We could feel the Holy Spirit's presence very strongly while worshiping and during our time of fellowship.

On the same day, our dear friends Tony and Fernanda Portigliatti scheduled a meeting at his house with an oncologist friend of his to talk with us. He also invited some friends in common to pray with us and seek God's direction regarding my situation. Dr. A.S. was a Brazilian oncologist who was living in Boca Raton with his family at that time. They came that afternoon to talk with us and helped us interpret my results, explaining in more detail the stage of the lymphoma.

He also talked about research that he was doing about strengthening the immune system. The entire group listened carefully to the results of his research. We called an American missionary in Brazil who had fibromyalgia and had used Immunocal. My husband, Dr. A.S., and the rest of the group traced a road map for me to prepare for the treatment. We also had a time of prayer together. Two days later, I began taking it to strength my immune system.

That week was like a spiritual retreat for us. God sent David so we could worship together as well as the Willis family and Dr. A.S.. Everyone had their own role in blessing us at this specific time in our lives. We didn't know what was coming our way, but the Father was showing His unfailing love and care for us every day during that time of struggle.

That same week Cliff came to visit our prayer meeting on Friday night. It was wonderful to have him with us, and once more Father God visited us with His manifested presence. All these acts of love were like water in a desert land for us. It was a time to refresh our souls.

O God, You are my God; early will I seek You; my soul thirsts for You; my flesh longs for You in a dry and thirsty land where there is no water (Psalms 63:1).

THE ACTION PLAN: WE NEED WARRIORS IN THE FIELD

One week after I began taking the supplement for my immune system, I went to my first visit to the oncologist—the first of many.

At this point, our relatives and close friends began to hear what we were going through, and I was flooded with e-mails, phone calls, suggestions, tips, words of encouragement, and comfort. Some of them didn't know what to say and remained silent. All of them prayed.

I remembered what my cousin from Rio de Janeiro told me when she had been going through a tough time in her life once. She had suggested building an action plan, designating one person of the family to do a specific task, starting with the two of us—my husband and me. We decided that my husband would filter all the information, e-mails, and phone calls that were related to getting people's information or their concerns about my situation. I would receive information only from those who could help me build my faith and hope for my future, keeping my eyes focused on the Father's eyes. At the same time, I did not want to be ignorant of what was going on.

What happens in situations like this is that some people, although they have good intentions, don't know how to help or speak. Many times in an effort to be what they think is realistic, they express themselves in a way that is not appropriate, and that doesn't help those who are going through a hard time and seeking to maintain a stand of faith and hope. If a message was delivered with a negative connotation instead of the positive one intended, it did not help us. In reality, we knew what was going on and the risks, but we were not only going through a physical battle but an emotional and mental one as well. Filtering what I heard helped us position our faith where it needed to be—in the Father God and the healing that comes from Him. This was one of many decisions in which my husband took a heroic stand.

It was not easy for us to find an oncologist in a city where we didn't know many people. It was a big challenge because we had never had a need for such a specialist before. In the beginning, we didn't know where to start. We felt totally in God's hands. We decided to start with the oncologist our primary doctor recommended. February 22nd was my first visit. We heard a lot of new information that would take some time to digest. We liked the doctor, but we didn't like the way his staff treated us. We felt that we were just one more patient on their list of many—just a number, and we didn't like it. We were expecting care and love. The situation was already stressful, and we didn't want to deal with a lack of care at the same time. Feeling disappointed, we decided that we would try to find another doctor.

That same week, my husband contacted the doctor our new friend from our divine appointment suggested. It is so hard to describe in words what was going on with us. Sometimes we felt that we were dreaming and would wake up soon. Other times we had the feeling that we were part of a movie and that this was not really happening. It was a battle in our minds, and our faith was challenged every day. We trusted that God was with us at all times, guiding and giving us directions, but in truth the mental battle was huge.

That weekend we went to Jacksonville to meet some friends at a Zadok Fellowship meeting led by missionary Dan Duke. It was very refreshing and comforting for us to participate in that meeting with dear brothers and sisters in Christ. The worship and fellowship were a blessing. During the time of fellowship, I felt that what we were going through was not that big. When you hear people of God sharing their experiences, you discover that your problem is not that hard.

My hope was strengthened and revitalized. I heard many testimonies of healing and recovering and how God carried each person who was in need of a miracle like us. With hearts filled with faith, our perspective changed even more. This "mountain" was not that impossible to overcome. Encouraged, I thought, "If God did all this for these brothers and sisters, He will do it for me too." I agreed with heaven. We had an entire weekend in which we felt the Father comforting us. Now we had to wait to see what the next step was.

On Monday after this wonderful weekend, I received the results of the pathology exams from Mayo Clinic. The report confirmed the diagnosis given by the Florida hospital—Hodgkin's lymphoma. Lymphomas are cancers that start in white blood cells called lymphocytes. The lymph system is part of the immune system, which helps fight infections and some other diseases. It also helps the flow of fluids in the body. The most common symptom of Hodgkin's lymphoma is a lump in the neck, under the arm, or in the groin, which is an enlarged lymph node.[1]

Now I had two comparison exams on hand. At that point, I didn't know the impact that this piece of paper would have in the future. That same week I had a CT scan to have a better idea of the situation. I waited for that for weeks. The clock was ticking and we needed to start treatment quickly. We also hadn't found an oncologist yet. My family in Brazil was very concerned about the time that was passing fast. This pressure did not help.

ENDNOTES:

1- "What is Hodgkin Lymphoma?" (2017). *American Cancer Society.* Retrieved on April 28, 2017, from https://www.cancer.org/cancer/hodgkin-lymphoma/detection-diagnosis-staging/signs-and-symptoms.html

Part 2
The Healing Rain

Four

HEALING RAIN

There are events in our lives that mark us forever. One day at work, while on my break, I started my walk by asking God some questions and trying to reason through this whole ordeal I was going through. At that time, I hadn't started the chemotherapy. I was asking God why all these things were happening to me. I was anxious and stressed about what I was going through.

Suddenly, Michael W. Smith's song "*Healing Rain*"[1] came into my mind and I began to sing the chorus:

Healing rain is falling down,

Healing rain is falling down,

I'm not afraid.

I'm not afraid.

I opened my arms in the middle of the parking in lot, closed my eyes, and sang. I felt the warmth of God's embrace and my heart yielded to Him. I began to believe He was more than enough to heal me. The spiritual rain from heaven was falling over me in that hour. It was a remarkable experience—a moment of surrender and trust that changed my life that I will never forget. I thought to myself, *"Why should I be afraid if I am hidden in His love?"* The apostle John said:

> *There is no fear in love; but perfect love casts out fear, because fear involves torment. But he who fears has not been made perfect in love* (1 John 4:18).

This was exactly what I felt when I sang this song. If God had already promised me that He took all my infirmities with Him to the cross then I had an assurance in my heart that allowed me to sing with conviction that *"healing rain is coming down"* and *"I am not afraid."*

From that moment on, I sang this song every moment that I felt I needed His embrace. In other words, every day. It is amazing how God uses a song, a person, a book, His Word, actually anything to talk with us. We just need to pay attention to these things and take the time to hear from Him.

I am very thankful to those who obey the Holy Spirit when He whispers songs, messages, or assignments into their ears. We never know what can happen when we do that. God always surprises us by going above our expectations. Thank you, Michael W. Smith, for writing this song and Z88.3, our local radio station, for playing this music.

ENDNOTES:

1. Michael W. Smith, writer, "Healing Rain," Michael W. Smith, Reunion Records, 2004, CD.

Part 3
The Preparation

The Second Consequence of the Divine Encounter

Five

THE SECOND CONSEQUENCE OF THE DIVINE ENCOUNTER

Divine encounters happen is the most unlikely places. An example is the day I had both CT and PET scans in order to determine the stage of the disease. In between these scans I received some visitors who came to our house to encourage us.

Finally, on February 10th we were able to visit Dr. S. at the Moffitt Cancer Center, who had been referred to us by our divinely appointed doctor from the Miami airport. The cancer center was a one-hour drive from Orlando. We made plans to work during the morning and drive there around noon. My husband picked me up at work and we worshiped and prayed all the way there. Our hearts were full of gratitude for the opportunity that God was giving us to visit this doctor. It does not sound rational, but we were having a supernatural experience.

One of our prayers was that God would give us direction on the right place for treatment. If it was with Dr. S., who was the head of a research team and a specialist in lymphoma and suggested by our new friend from the Mayo Clinic, we asked God that the doctor himself would say this right from the beginning. Otherwise, that Dr. S. would recommend another doctor and place for me to do the treatment.

We arrived there earlier than planned. We decided to have some lunch before the visit right there in the car in front of the hospital. We were talking about many things. Suddenly, I look at the hospital façade; it read *Moffitt Cancer Center*. At that moment something happened inside of me. I realized that I was not there to visit somebody or pray for someone. I was there as a patient. I was shocked. I also noticed that during our time there, I did not see any young people coming in or out of those doors. I felt too young to be there and too young to be going through this. I mentioned my feelings to my husband, friend, and partner who was present with me all the time. I needed his strength and encouragement. We decided to pray to the Father to give me peace in my heart and give me grace to deal with this. We praised the Lord and declared that I was embracing the healing that God had already given me.

After that time of prayer in the parking lot, we checked in to the hospital. Now I was on the other side, a patient, and it felt quite strange. As a designer, I naturally noticed the surrounding area in the lobby. I was not only paying attention to aspects of the building but also the people. There were all kinds of people there—new patients, others in treatment, some accompanied by an acquaintance. My heart overflowed with compassion toward them. Some questions came to my mind: "What I am doing here?" and "What will be my future?" The battle in my mind was strong. I started to speak in tongues to edify my spirit. It helped me to focus on the Father's eyes. At the same time, questions poured into my mind. I never felt abandoned by God. I had peace in my inner man. It was like a paradox. I knew God was there with me and that He knew what was going on in my mind and heart as I sat and waited to go into the doctor's office.

After being led to a room to wait further, we paused for a minute, looked at each other, and realized we didn't have a lot to say. Instead, we started to declare what the Bible says that we are. We were setting the atmosphere, asking for discernment and direction. The doctor opened the door and ushered in a group of medical students with him. What an odd feeling. This was a lot of people to be looking at me all at the same time. I felt a little bit intimidated.

The first question that he asked was, "Who recommended me?" When I said that it was somebody from Mayo Clinic, he couldn't hide his happiness. He had a big smile. From that moment on, we realized that every time we produced the pathology report from Mayo Clinic, the doctors would treat us differently. They would give us more attention than before. We knew God had provided that divine appointment because He knew we would need this. This was just one more demonstration of His divine love and care toward us. It was the favor of God.

Just after this introduction, he said that he could recommend oncologists in the Orlando area, so we didn't need to drive to Tampa for treatment. This statement itself was an answer to our prayers. We didn't ask for the information, but just as we had prayed, the doctor offered it first. Dr. S. and his team gave us a lot of attention and answered all our questions. He was very clear about the type of treatment that he performed. His treatment was more on the traditional side, and we preferred using a holistic process as well. We decided to take his recommendations and visit an oncologist in the Orlando area too.

We left there happy because we knew that our quest for the right oncologist was narrowing down. At the same time, Dr. S. confirmed that I had stage two of Hodgkin's lymphoma, which was located on my neck and chest. In addition, he also mentioned that I might have to follow a protocol that would include chemotherapy and radiation. Now we had to process all this and continue to seek God's guidance to find the right place to be treated.

THE JOURNEY TO FIND TREATMENT CONTINUES

As soon as we arrived in Orlando, my husband contacted a doctor in the area suggested by Dr. S. The first of the list had moved to another city. The second name was Dr. J.S. from MD Anderson Cancer Center. The time was going too fast and our family was pressuring us to start treatment quickly. We knew the urgency. There were a lot of things going on at the same time. We had a lot to learn and respond to in such a short period of time.

I remember talking about my situation to a doctor in Brazil; she had recommended going to MD Anderson in Houston, Texas. It was the first time I had heard about the hospital. The doctor we were scheduled to visit was from the same institution, so I decided to do some research on the Internet. I didn't even know that MD Anderson had a branch in Orlando then. It was a surprise to me. I remember saying to myself, "Maybe that is the place I am supposed to go for treatment."

THE NEW DECISION

The day of my visit arrived. Finally, we felt at peace with everything that was discussed. We had found a place to begin treatment. We liked Dr. J.S. and his team. That same day, we planned my journey for the next three months. I still had to go to Brazil to take care of some personal things. Dr. J.S. agreed, and gave us two weeks. We saw God open doors for us as we found a last-minute ticket over the Easter holiday.

Before I left, I had to complete a series of tests for my heart, lungs, and bone marrow, just to name a few. The last one was one day before our trip. It was a little bit painful to sit in an airplane for nine hours after the bone marrow test, but we made it.

Six

THE SUPPORT TEAM ARRIVES!

Two weeks later, we were back in Orlando and my parents were with us. They put aside all their activities and volunteered to help us for the first three months.

First thing, I had more tests and a surgery to put in a port on my chest. This port is a small disc made of plastic or metal that sits under the skin. A soft, thin tube called a catheter connects the port to a large vein. The chemotherapy drugs are given through a special needle that fits right into the port.[1] I didn't have time to rest because I had to work at the same time. An avalanche was taking place in our lives. We were in need of prayer and the grace of God. Our Friday night prayer meetings started on that Friday, and it was so good to participate in those meetings.

On this same Friday, I took my first dose of chemotherapy. It was quite a challenge because I had no idea what would happen. I was trying to focus totally on God's support. Those who accompanied me were also anxious about this new journey. In a special way, I was telling my mom and dad that everything was going to be all right. During the waiting, we talked about many other things besides what we were doing there. It was good. This whole event was new for us, and we didn't know how to react. We were trying to be as normal as we could.

THE GOODNESS OF GOD

When the nurse called me, we all got silent. I went with my husband into the treatment room. Our nurse was very receptive and full of joy. I liked that. She could tell by my countenance that this was my first time there and she was very kind to explain how to play "this game" right in order to win. God was using Liz (my first nurse) to bring me faith and hope. Later on, I discovered that she was a Christian.

My spirit was lifted, even though I was also asking God why I was going through all this and what His plans were. I didn't know all the answers to my questions, but one thing I knew and embraced—His goodness and mercy was following me every day of my life (see Psalms 23:6). He was unfolding my destiny one day at a time, and He was there for me.

I left the hospital after four hours of chemotherapy. I felt good, ready to go somewhere or do something. We probably did something light that day and then went home. The next day I slept every time I felt like I needed to rest. Within 48 hours of my first dose, some side effects began to kick in. For some hours, I felt the strangest thing. I could not look straight forward for some hours. It stopped after some weeks but was very uncomfortable. My oncologist had never heard of this side effect before. Everybody has a different reaction while in treatment. It is very hard to predict.

A LITTLE BREAK

The following week I returned to work and had my weekend off from the hospital. So far, I was fine. We decided to go out with my parents because they were here. We took them to Lake Eola and others part of Orlando. We were simply trying to have a normal life as much as we could. We were trying to focus our attention on other things rather than the treatment. From then on, we started regarding simple things in life with a different meaning.

WE NEED HIS PRESENCE

Our Friday prayer meeting continued to be a place of rest for my soul. This was true not just for me but for everybody in my house. It was a place where the presence of God would come to visit, comfort, restore, and speak to us. Sometimes it was a place where we had to fight, cry, and call things into existence. These meetings were vital.

There is nothing that we can do without God's presence. After an encounter with the Father, we change. Our values, perspectives, and goals change. During this time, we saw God revealing Himself as a Father more than any other time in our life—a Father who cares and is present all the time. All four of us were changing more into His likeness every time that we met Him during these meetings. It is hard to put into words things that are so personal and intimate, but every person needs to experience this.

> *You make known to me the path of life; you will fill me with joy in your presence, with eternal pleasures at your right hand* (Psalms 16:11 NIV).

ENDNOTES:

1. "How is Chemotherapy Given?" (2015), *Breastcancer.org*. Retrieved on April 28, 2017, from http://www.breastcancer.org/treatment/chemotherapy/process/how.

Seven

SECOND CHEMO

My second week after chemo was better. I worked all week and went to the doctor to take out my stitches from the surgery. I was healing.

Friday arrived and I prepared as much as I could to go to the next round of chemo. Before they give a person a chemotherapy, the take a blood cell count to make sure everything is as it should be. After my blood test, I was informed that I couldn't take the drugs. My white blood cells were so low that the nurse looked at me and said, "Are you feeling anything?" and I said, "No." She said, "Your white cell count is so low that you should not be here without a mask or without some type of reaction." I was surprised because I had taken my parents to visit a trade show that I was working at the day before. I had been in the midst of a multitude of people and didn't know that I couldn't be there. God was taking care of me.

I was sent home and had to wait until the next week, so my body had some time to recover from the first chemo.

What an adventure! We didn't know anything about any of this and we were learning something new every day.

THOUGHTS

Life is something. Sometimes we are walking in one direction and suddenly something hits us. During this "crash" the best question to ask is, "What does God wants to teach me with that?" and not "Why, God?" Our reaction dictates the next step in pursuing our goal.

He leads me in the paths of righteousness for His name's sake (Psalms 23:3).

MOTHER'S DAY

Now Mother's Day was around the corner. Every moment counted, and we needed to seize what we could. I didn't know what was going to happen tomorrow, so I planned to enjoy every day. I had not celebrated Mother's Day with my mom for many years. It was wonderful to have her with us, so we wanted to make it extra special.

We decided to take her to lunch at her favorite restaurant and surprised her with a card. I could see in her eyes how much this meant to her. Family is very important, and it is in moments like this that we build good memories that last forever in our minds. God creates us to be His family and to live in family. We feel this strong connection in the depths of our hearts.

Honor your father and your mother, so that you may live long in the land the Lord your God is giving you (Exodus 20:12 NIV).

SECOND DOSE AGAIN

After taking a vaccine to boost my white cells I went for the second dose of chemo. My counts were reasonable enough to proceed with the treatment. And so it went—one more time spending hours in the hospital taking the drugs.

It was my husband's birthday and we celebrated it during our prayer meeting, praising the Father for his life. He had a cake on the following day even though I slept almost all day. It was not the type of birthday that I would have liked to give him, but both of us were thankful to spend that day together, alive one more year.

The recovery after the second dose was harder than before. My body was starting to get used to the amount of drugs in it, so every chemo had different reactions. It was an adjustment phase with a lot of ups and downs.

ADJUSTMENT

Sometimes it is hard to adjust to a new phase, especially when you don't expect the changes and they are not exactly the kind you had hoped for and dreamt about. In cases like that, the best thing to do is to run toward the Father. David said:

> *The Lord is near to those who have a broken heart, and saves such as have a contrite spirit* (Psalms 34:18).

"And you shall know the truth, and truth shall make you free."
John 8:32

Part 4
Nuggets of Truth

DOVE'S EYES

I was doing my best to prepare physically and mentally for the third dose of chemo. We decided it was a good idea to spend the weekend in a city close by, just to break down our "hospital to home to work" routine.

In the meantime, we took the opportunity to celebrate my birthday. For me it was more significant than ever. Many things were going on in my mind that day. I was thankful, but at the same time I was wondering about my next birthday. I confess that I felt a battle in my mind concerning my future.

Basically, I had to choose between two thoughts—life or death. I chose to have "dove's eyes." Misty Edwards, from the International House of Prayer in Kansas City (IHOPKC), wrote a song from Song of Solomon; one of the lines said, *"Give me dove's eyes; give me undistracted devotion for only You."*[1] In that moment, what I really needed was to keep my eyes on the eyes of the Father and not let anything distract me from that relationship. It didn't matter what was ahead of me.

I needed to sustain an undistracted devotion toward God. I believed in His promises and His thoughts toward me, and this comforted me.

> *For I know the thoughts that I think toward you, says the Lord, thoughts of peace and not of evil, to give you a future and a hope* (Jeremiah 29:11).

I embraced this verse with all of my heart, knowing that whatever was happening, God was carrying me all the time.

> *I will instruct you and teach you in the way you should go; I will guide you with My eye* (Psalms 32:8).

THIRD DOSE: TRUST AND REST

Although I was preparing for the third dose, it didn't happen. My white cell count was low again. There was nothing I could do. It was the second time that I had to skip chemo. The weekend was followed by a holiday, and we decided to stay at home and rest. Actually, it was not a "rest" because at the same time we were preparing to move to another home and some of our relatives were planning to visit. The many preparations were a good distraction for our minds, so we didn't have to focus on the treatment and my situation.

One of the things that I learned with this experience was that when you are in a battle, like my body was, there are moments when you can't do much. You have to trust in God and rest. Most of the time, at least for me with my restless spirit, this was not an easy thing to do. I needed the help of the Holy Spirit to teach me about these subjects.

Jesus was my biggest example of trust. Isaiah 53:5 says, "*But He was wounded for our transgressions, He was bruised for our iniquities; the chastisement for our peace was upon Him, and by His stripes we are healed."* He knew what was going to happen to Him during his journey on earth, and He trusted the Father all the time, regardless of the circumstances. His act of surrender has always astounded me. He knew what was coming, but He didn't know the extent of the pain He would have to endure as a human. The scars He received during His time on earth, He will carry for eternity. I didn't know what was coming, and I had to keep my eyes on His eyes and surrender to Him, trusting in His promise to carry me through this dark season.

> *Yea, though I walk through the valley of the shadow of death, I will fear no evil; for You are with me; Your rod and Your staff, they comfort me* (Psalms 23:4).

> *In God have I put my trust: I will not be afraid what man can do unto me* (Psalms 56:11 KJV).

SURPRISE BELOW THE CARPET

In addition to the treatments and the arrival of our guests from Brazil, we were moving into a new house. We had a lot happening all at the same time. I don't do well with carpet, so we knew we wanted to replace the carpeting with a wood floor. My husband and my daddy decided to take out the brand-new carpet and prepare the floor for the new finish.

To our surprise, when they started to pull out the carpet they found a beautiful, brand-new flooring surface with construction dust all over it. Now their job was to make sure this surface was totally clean.

Many times, we judge situations, people, or circumstances too quickly. Take that carpet. When I first arrived at the house and looked at it, the carpet was clean, had that brand-new carpet smell, and a beautiful appearance. But the dust resided just below the surface.

Between the first and third doses of chemo, I skipped treatment two times because my white cell count was too low. Even though I couldn't feel anything different, that could be a sign of what was going on with my body. The battle was there and I didn't know it. My body was armed and fighting with all it had as well as the drugs that were coming in. We need discernment to see beyond the surface. The Holy Spirit gives us this discernment.

I am your servant; give me discernment that I may understand your statutes (Psalms 119:125 NIV).

The fear of the Lord is the beginning of wisdom, and knowledge of the Holy One is understanding (Proverbs 9:10 NIV).

THE SOURCE

The next couple of weeks we had everything together—the move was done, the guests started coming and going, the treatment was on pace now for the first time without skipping dates. I was also able to continue working as normally as possible.

My recovery time was between three- to three-and-a-half days. Slowly all the weirdness that I was feeling after forty-eight hours of taking chemo was gone. It was the strangest feeling that I ever experienced in my life. It was very uncomfortable.

I slept a lot during the weekends. Every time I felt tired or I needed rest, I slept a little bit. On the other hand, I was able to go out sometimes to do something with my visiting family. It was very nice that they could come. We talked about many subjects that distracted me from the treatment and it was very good for our minds. Another thing that was distracting me was putting my house in order after our move. All these events helped us feel that we were living a "normal" life.

We had to reschedule all the first tests because of the delay on the treatment. At this point I was almost in the middle of the chemo treatments. My oncologist suggested that maybe I could finish chemo earlier than was expected. The news gave me hope, but I had to undergo a set of tests first to see how my body was really responding.

My body started to yield to the fact that every two weeks I would receive a dose of the chemo cocktail. Slowly, I was getting weaker; my energy level was decreasing. I had to focus on God who was my source of hope, love, and faith and not allow my mind be a hostage to fear.

"The power (of God) does not bow to the panic, but rather, the assurance of its source." —Rita Springer

I love what Rita Springer wrote because the power of God is so beyond our understanding and above all things. The God I trust, the God who wove me in the womb of my mother (see Psalms 139:13), the God who created all the universe and placed sea, sky, trees, and land in its place with His power was carrying me through this dark season of my life, all the way through, and He smiled at me.

How could I be angry about this? No, I was thankful for His promises. Yes, there were many questions that I could not answer, but I put them aside and focused my eyes on His eyes—the source of life. Dove's eyes!

For You formed my inward parts; You covered me in my mother's womb. I will praise You, for I am fearfully and wonderfully made; marvelous are Your works, and that my soul knows very well (Psalms 139:13-14).

ENDNOTES:
1. Misty Edwards, *Dove's Eyes*, Misty Edwards, Forerunner Music, 2007, CD.

Nine

CHEERFUL HEART

A cheerful heart is good medicine, but a crushed spirit dries up the bones (Proverbs 17:22 NIV).

Solomon understood the importance of having a cheerful heart. It brings health not just for our soul, but our body too. According to *Webster's Dictionary*, *cheerful* means: 1 a: full of good spirits, merry; "a cheerful host," b: ungrudging "cheerful obedience," 2: conducive to cheer; likely to dispel gloom or worry; "sunny cheerful room."[1]

Besides *cheerful* meaning "full of good spirits" and "likely to dispel gloom or worry," it also means "ungrudging" or *being without envy or reluctance.*[2] Reluctance is a struggle against something. If I am struggling against something, I will not have a cheerful heart, which is the medicine to my being. I needed to surrender my body and soul to God.

Did I need to stop fighting? If fighting meant to believe and keep my faith up, the answer is never; but if fighting was to resist the pursuit of a deeper understanding of the goodness and love of God, then the answer was (and is) yes. You have to stop being reluctant and stop building a wall of separation between you and God's love with your anger, dissatisfaction, hate, hesitancy, reticence, and unwillingness.

Surrender is a word that apparently doesn't fit in this circumstance. I am not talking about surrender to sickness. That is not the point here. I had to learn to yield to the power of God so the Holy Spirit could take control, not me. He needed to teach me to listen to His voice and believe in His care for me. I didn't stop commanding the sickness to go away; that was my duty, but in order to increase my faith and hope I had to be closer to Him, close enough to hear His voice.

THE ELEMENT OF SURPRISE

In order to engage in warfare you have to use one principle: the element of surprise. According to Robert R. Leonhard in an article published in *Armchair General* magazine:

> *Surprise results from the combination of two elements. The first is time. Surprise is a temporal phenomenon, and it makes no sense to think about surprise unless we keep it in its context of time. Surprise occurs when one side "turns the time flank" of the other side.*
>
> *The other element of surprise is perpetual unreadiness. Military organizations are perpetually unready for combat. Unreadiness is the normal condition of all combatants. Suppose that the enemy knows that an attack is imminent. He therefore takes extreme measures to ready his forces for battle. The problem is that he can prepare only for what he can anticipate. Techniques for delaying the enemy's detection*

include using stealth, camouflage, deception, operational security measure, and the indirect approach. An ambush, aims to overwhelm the enemy not just with weapons fire, but also with confusion, noise and fear.

Surprise, then, is a principle of war that is alive and well. It is an enduring feature of warfare, because its components— time and perpetual unreadiness— are immutable. Just as they have done throughout history, commanders will continue to seek ways to delay detection, hasten contact, and vary the method of attack in order to expose the enemy's unreadiness, turn the enemy's time flank, and win.[3]

In my case, the element of surprise was also related to time and readiness. Time was related when I didn't skip any of our prayer meetings even though they were on the same day I had chemo. Readiness was rising in worship to the Father during those meetings. It was critical that I be there, seeking God's presence and being embraced by His arms of love. What a precious moment when my husband began to prophesy, singing and playing his guitar. God visited us. Sometimes we were on the floor, sometimes we were standing or even kneeling, but the most important thing was this— He always showed up. Those experiences were like fuel to my spirit, granting me the power to endure the next round. Experiencing God's goodness and love was key for us in that unique journey.

We knew that the enemy was against us positioning ourselves to radically worship God with all we had. However, our eyes were on Jesus, the beloved of our souls. Every meeting was different. To this very day, we get together to worship Him every Friday night.

Being engaged in God's presence with a cheerful heart will make the enemy fearful. Now the game had changed. We were not the ones who were full of fear, the enemy was. The spirit of infirmity needed to flee in Jesus' name because we had positioned ourselves by yielding to His love. That brought us faith and hope.

LAUGHING

Speaking of the element of surprise, I can say that laughter is a very good strategy. Many times in our prayer and worship meetings, we had moments when we felt a wave of joy coming from God, one we could not explain. It was a supernatural feeling that was pouring out from heaven to us. We left those meetings feeling good.

On March 7, 2005, the results of this study, conducted at the University of Maryland Medical Center, were presented at the Scientific Session of the American College of Cardiology in Orlando, Florida. The study said that:

> *Watching a funny film boosts the way blood vessels function. Stress caused blood flow to slow by around 35%, but laughter increased it by around 22%, they told the American College of Cardiology.*
>
> *Michael Miller, director of preventive cardiology at the University of Maryland Medical Center, who led the research, said: "The endothelium is the first line in the development of atherosclerosis or hardening of the arteries, so, given the results of our study, it is conceivable that laughing may be important to maintain a healthy endothelium, and reduce the risk of cardiovascular disease.*

> "At the very least, laughter offsets the impact of mental stress, which is harmful to the endothelium." He added: "Thirty minutes of exercise three times a week, and 15 minutes of laughter on a daily basis is probably good for the vascular system."[4]

Also, according with Melinda Smith, M.A., and Jeanne Segal, Ph.D.:

> *Humor and laughter strengthen your immune system, boost your energy, diminish pain, and protect you from the damaging effects of stress. Best of all, this priceless medicine is fun, free, and easy to use.*[5]

One of my goals during the treatment was to boost my immune system. Everyone in my house was doing their own research about how to do that. We found great supplements like Immunocal and certain types of foods, but laughter was the best one. I remember a comment that my mom made when we were going through some pictures: "We are always smiling in the photos. Nobody would know what we were going through if they just saw these pictures." She was right. Everybody was smiling; there were no sad faces. We could not explain why that was. The only possibility is that it was God's supernatural mercy and goodness. I was walking through the darkest valley of my life, and for some reason I experienced waves of joy during our prayer meetings. Our pictures show us smiling. Go figure! God works through mysteries!

> *You have turned for me my mourning into dancing; You have put off my sackcloth and clothed me with gladness* (Psalms 30:11).

Splendor and majesty are before him; strength and joy are in his dwelling place (1 Chronicles 16:27 NIV).

Our mouths were filled with laughter, our tongues with songs of joy. Then it was said among the nations, "The Lord has done great things for them" (Psalms 126:2 NIV).

ENDNOTES:

1. Cheerful. In *Merriam-Webster.com*. Retrieved on April 28, 2017, from https://www.merriam-webster.com/dictionary/cheerful

2. Ungrudging. In *Merriam-Webster.com*. Retrieved on April 28, 2017, from https://www.merriam-webster.com/dictionary/ungrudging

3. Leonhard. R., (n.d.). Surprise. *Armchair General*. Retrieved from http://www.jhuapl.info/ourwork/nsa/papers/surprise.pdf

4. Seiler, B., (2005). School of medicine study show laughter helps blood vessels function better. *University of Maryland Medical Center*. Retrieved from http://www.umm.edu/news-and-events/news-releases/2005/school-of-medicine-study-shows-laughter-helps-blood-vessels-function-better

5. Robinson, L., Smith, M., & Segal, J., (2017). Laughter is the best medicine. *Helpguide.org*. Retrieved from https://www.helpguide.org/articles/emotional-health/laughter-is-the-best-medicine.htm

Ten

DON'T POSSESS DISEASES

My oncologist mentioned that I could stop chemo if all of my first set of tests after the beginning of the treatment were fine. We still had guests at our house. On one hand, it was good for everybody because we could talk, laugh, and have quality time as a family. I sometimes went for solitary walks and other times went places with everybody, but my primary focus was on resting as much as I could. The drugs were draining me of my energy.

Two days after the sixth chemo, I had a fever and I was not feeling well at all. The day was long for me. My CT scan and heart test were scheduled for that week. I remember it like it was yesterday. When I entered the room to do my heart test, a young nurse began asking me that entire list of questions as always. She asked me why I was there. I promptly answered her, "I really don't know, but my doctor said that I need to come here." She smiled and continued asking what my cancer was. I turned to her and said, "I don't have cancer, but I was diagnosed with Hodgkin's lymphoma."

She looked at me, paused for a few seconds, awe clearly written on her face, and said, "I like your attitude. I wish all my patients had an attitude like yours." Then she smiled and began the test.

One thing that I never did was declare that I possessed this disease. Sometimes people say things without thinking, like, "My cancer, my diabetes, my sickness." Those words take possession of something.

In English grammar, *my* is classified as a pronoun, a possessive determiner:

Possessive determiners are a type of function word used in front of a noun to express possession or belonging (ownership).[1]

I don't own a cancer. It is illegal and it has to leave. I was not created to be sick. I was created to reflect God's glory. Jesus Christ already took the burden of sickness upon Himself on the cross about 2,000 years ago, and I decided to believe and receive His word into my life. That illness was illegal in my body.

And with the stripes [that wounded] Him we are healed and made whole (Isaiah 53:5 AMPC).

What an act of love Isaiah describes here. I decided to embrace this verse all the way during my journey and declared these words every day. The circumstances didn't matter. The truth did.

I still had two more tests—the PET and another for my lungs. The drugs that I was taking could have affected my heart and lungs, so they needed to be monitored.

BETWEEN HAPPINESS AND UNCERTAINTY

Finally the day for the seventh chemo arrived, followed by a doctor's visit. I was hoping to hear that everything was well and I could stop chemo. Every dose was making me lose energy.

Dr. J.S. looked at my exams (with a drumroll I could almost hear) and told me that I was clean. The main mass of the tumor had shrunk significantly. I was very happy with the news, but then he added, "In order to consolidate the treatment, I want you to take one more set of the drugs and finish the cycle." Well, that meant five more doses. I was not so sure I liked this part of the conversation. Even though he suspended two of the four drugs so as to not affect my lungs any further, it was still a long way left to go. My heart test said that the organ was remarkable. That was great news too.

I left the doctor's office with a mixture of happiness and uncertainty. My heart was glad for the fact that my body was clean of any cancer cells, and I thanked God for His goodness and mercy. On the other hand, I had to focus on the doses that were ahead of me. I made a new countdown list, so every time I had chemo I crossed one off the list. That helped me see that my finish line was getting closer. It was time to regroup, reevaluate, and trace a new plan.

ENDNOTES:

1. Nordquist, R., (2017). Possessive determiner in English grammar. *ThoughtCo*. Retrieved from https://www.thoughtco.com/possessive-determiner-grammar-1691648

Dealing with Fear

DEALING WITH FEAR

Many times in life we face fear. During my journey, I had many battles with this enemy. There were many situations that triggered fear, like stress, trauma, unknown situations, and so on. Now I was facing another. What would it mean to go through five more doses of chemo and one month of radiation?

According to the article Julia Layton wrote titled "How Fear Works":

> *Fear is a chain reaction in the brain that starts with a stressful stimulus and ends with the release of chemicals that cause a racing heart, fast breathing and energized muscles, among other things, also known as the fight-or-flight response. The stimulus could be a spider, a knife at your throat, an auditorium full of people waiting for you to speak or the sudden thud of your front door against the door frame.*[1]

You can't predict when you will feel fear. Most times it is involuntary and can freeze your reactions. However, you can overcome fear by knowing who you are in God.

Here is a quote from Kris Vallotton about fear:

> *Fear is a serial killer, the prime suspect in the death of more people on the planet than all other diseases combined. Fear in every form has been linked to heart disease, cancer, autoimmune disorders, mental illness and many other sicknesses. Fear is the welcome mat to demonic activity in our lives. The prophet Isaiah wrote, "You will be far from oppression, for you will not fear..." (Isaiah 54:14). When we reject fear, we live in peace. But if we allow fear to creep into our lives, we soon find ourselves oppressed, tormented and tortured.*
>
> *Nehemiah's cure for his people's anxiety was simply to "remember the Lord who is great and awesome." Fear dismembers and disfigures our perspective of God, making Him a powerless pawn, controlled by our circumstances. But when we remember the Lord and re-count His works, we begin to re-form our vision of His greatness in our hearts. As we meditate on His greatness, confidence begins to sprout in the soil of faith and soon fear's fantasy is unmasked, flogged and sent fleeing.[2]*

One of the things that I would like to point out from Kris's quote is that remembering God's greatness reframes our perspective of Him and helps us overcome fear. How will we remember His awesomeness? By meditating on His Word and spending time with Him in prayer and worship—building relationship. As I grow in relationship with Him, I think and believe as He does. *"For as he thinks in his heart, so is he"* (Prov. 23:7). In addition, it is wonderful to know that His thoughts about me are thoughts of peace to give me a future and hope.

> *"For I know the plans I have for you," says the Lord. "They are plans for good and not for disaster, to give you a future and*

a hope" (Jeremiah 29:11 NLT).

As our relationship with Father God grows, our trust in His love will grow as well. Our "real" identity in Him starts to be revealed during these moments with Him. By knowing Him, we know the Father. The Holy Spirit expands this revelation in our hearts and mind.

> *I love what John says: "There is no fear in love [dread does not exist], but full-grown (complete, perfect) love turns fear out of doors and expels every trace of terror! For fear brings with it the thought of punishment, and [so] he who is afraid has not reached the full maturity of love [is not yet grown into love's complete perfection]"* (1 John 4:18 AMPC, emphasis mine).

Our love must grow in maturity, so we can be secure in our real identity and see from God's perspective. During our time with the Father, we should ask Him to reveal to us how He sees us. When we start doing this, our paradigm will completely change. His love toward us is so deep, so immense that it is hard to understand it.

Throughout the last phase of the treatment, I was pressing on toward getting to know Him more. I realized how tangible His love was in my inner man; I was feeling His love and goodness in a way that I never experienced before. I embraced the idea of waking up every morning, knowing that He would satisfy me with His unfailing love.

> *Satisfy us in the morning with your unfailing love, that we may sing for joy and be glad all our days* (Psalms 90:14 NIV).

And this same love is unshakable.

"Though the mountains be shaken and the hills be removed, yet my unfailing love for you will not be shaken nor my covenant of peace be removed," says the Lord, who has compassion on you (Isaiah 54:10 NIV).

What a good way to start a day when you know that everything that is coming is so unpredictable. Fear is an enemy that needs to be defeated, and you do this with love. Love always wins.

Don't fear the darkness or the pressure of the high places. Fear God and let Him take you into spheres beyond your current ability.[3]

THE UNPREDICTABLE HAPPENED

What can we do when the unpredictable happens during an unexpected situation? I was already going through an unexpected situation, and now something else crossed my path. Between the eighth and ninth doses, two important things happened. One of them was celebrating Father's Day with my father. I had not had this opportunity for many years. It was so good to have him here with us. We had a good time together.

The other was that I fell in the aisle of a supermarket and cut my knee with a piece of glass. On my weekend off from the hospital, I decided to do some shopping. I was very happy with that idea, because generally I was not strong enough to do this type of activity. Unfortunately, I slipped on the floor where a glass of tomato sauce had fallen before I arrived, and I ended up in a hospital again.

I could not believe that I was on the floor with my knee cut open. It was unthinkable. And there I was in the ER, waiting to get an x-ray. I was not aware that I had a piece of dirty glass under my skin. The doctor took the piece of glass out and closed the wound with four stitches. After a few hours in the hospital, I went home and could not go out the rest of the weekend.

When you are doing chemotherapy, you cannot have any cuts on your skin or any other place that could bring any kind of impurity into your body. Your immune system is already so busy fighting for your well-being that cuts or wounds will make it divide its attention. This situation brought consequences, but I was thankful to God that I didn't have to skip my next dose of chemotherapy. It took me a while to walk normally again and have everything healed on my knee, though.

God's mercy and goodness manifested one more time and we gave praises to Him in the midst of a challenging situation. The Bible speaks of people who went through similar situations. Daniel was a captive in Babylon who was inexpertly thrown into the lions' cave. Esther was already an orphan when she was captured to live in the palace, far from her closest family. Joseph was sold by his brothers to live in Pharaoh's house. In all of these situations, God carried them and gave them strength to go through trials. I had to believe and know that God was doing the same thing with me.

ENDNOTES:

1. Layton, J., (2005). How fear works. *HowStuffWorks Science*. Retrieved from http://science.howstuffworks.com/life/inside-the-mind/emotions/fear.htm

2. Vallotton, K., & Johnson, B., (2012). *Spirit Wars: Winning the Invisible Battle Against Sin and the Enemy.* Ada: Chosen Books.

3. Wallnau, Lance, (2013). Lance Wallnau. Retrieved from https://www.facebook.com/LanceWallnau/posts/10151956181249936?fref=nf

Twelve

RESTING PLACE WITHOUT STRIVING

Better is a handful with quietness than both hands full with painful effort, a vain striving after the wind and a feeding on it (Ecclesiastes 4:6 AMPC).

By now, I had three more doses of chemo to do and one month of radiation. I had been going to work at least four days a week up to this point. Many times, I took my work home. It was important for me to do some kind of activity. It kept me busy and not focused only on my health situation. However, sometimes I was really dragging in an effort to go to work, especially at the end of the treatments. I started to get weaker.

Just doing what I was doing was a miracle. Looking back, I don't know how I did so many things that year. I had to declare and command my soul and body every day to rise up, believing that I could do everything that I was supposed to do that day. It was not easy, and many times I asked my husband to do it for me so I could listen and exercise my faith.

God started to speak with me about dwelling in His resting place without striving to do things on my own. I am a very active person, so it was a challenge to understand how this could ever happen for me. I heard the Holy Spirit telling me to do some things, trusting in Him that He would take care of everything else. It was definitely a matter of trusting one hundred percent in Him and in His love toward me.

O Lord of hosts, blessed is the man who trusts in You!

(Psalms 84:12)

I started to change my mindset and began to let God take care of things for me instead of figuring everything out by myself. There was one particular nurse whom I liked the most during the treatment. Because nurses change shifts every week, I never knew when I would meet her again. Many times, I asked the Lord if that week I could have her as my nurse, and sure enough she would be there. Besides her great work as a nurse, she had a very good sense of humor and she was always smiling.

This small thing sounds very simple, I know, but God was teaching me something in my heart. I had many others, but the point is that I was learning to trust in Father God to take care of me. Surrender is a key word.

Beni Johnson said in her book *The Happy Intercessor* (which I highly recommend): *"Faith is more the product of surrender than it is to striving."*[1]

In addition, the *Merriam-Webster Dictionary* says that striving is *"to devote serious effort or energy and to struggle in opposition."*[2] And surrender is *"to give oneself up into the power of another; yield."*[3]

So it is better to surrender than to strive. Surrendering to His way of doing things and His will is not an inactive process but a shift of mindset. Our education system today has taught us to do something in order to be acceptable to someone. In other words, we have to labor, strive, or perform a thing so we can gain our identity. And who knows? We might even be accepted and loved by God then too. That is not what the Bible teaches us. In the kingdom of God, we start off accepted and loved. It is in that recognition and belief that our identity is formed. His desire for us is to believe and receive His love as well as to enter into His rest.

> *There remains therefore a rest for the people of God. For he who has entered His rest has himself also ceased from his works as God did from His* (Hebrews 4:9-10).

His rest is our place of refuge and peace. I began to learn this even more when I started to feel overwhelmed or I started striving, desiring something to happen. I needed to stop and go back to my resting place in my heart and mind; I had to find and maintain that place in Him. Once I am there, it does not matter what I am doing, but I feel peace and I live my life more fully and effectively in everything I do. It is an ongoing learning process that needs to be continually practiced and developed.

The shift of mindset comes when we learn to not just know but trust in and surrender to our source—God.

> *Except the Lord builds the house, they labor in vain who build it; except the Lord keeps the city, the watchman wakes but in vain. It is vain for you to rise up early, to take rest late,*

to eat the bread of [anxious] toil—for He gives [blessings] to His beloved in sleep (Psalms 127:1-2 AMPC, see also Psalms 121:1-5).

I read and meditated on these passages almost every day during that year. It was important for me to know that the Lord God was taking care of me while I slept. In fact, I slept a lot during this entire process. In the beginning, I was striving with myself not to sleep much, thinking that I was wasting my time or I could be doing something else. In fact, I had a sense of urgency that I needed to *do* something as much as I could to be healed. God brought to my attention that *He* was the One who was healing me while I was sleeping. He lovingly reminded me every day about this lesson that I was learning. He brought these verses to my attention every day as a fresh revelation of His care for me. My part was to learn to trust and surrender to His ways of taking care of me. I felt like He was embracing me as a Father, drawing me close to His chest, and telling me, *"Daughter, it is all right. I am taking care of you. You don't need to be anxious or strive anymore. I am here. Sleep well. I am taking care of everything for you."*

I can't emphasize enough that resting in God's love is a constant learning process. The image of God as Father grew significantly in me during this process. My desire is that this image grows in you too. The next question is: Can rest be developed in you? Is it a learning process too? Yes, it is.

Come to Me, all you who labor and are heavy laden, and I will give you rest. Take My yoke upon you and learn from Me, for I am gentle and lowly in heart, and you will find rest for your souls. For My yoke is easy and My burden is light (Matthew 11:28-30).

In this passage, Jesus is speaking about two ways of resting. The first one is when he says that *He will give us rest*. God gives us rest from circumstances, from our enemies, from many things that take us away from His presence. According to the *Hebrew-Greek Key Word Study Bible* (NIV),[4] the Greek word for *rest* in the first part of Matthew 11:28 has the same meaning as the word in Exodus 33:14. In the Old Testament, the corresponding Hebrew word for rest is *nûach* and means *to settle*, to be placed. God is taking us from a place of trouble and settling us in a place of rest.

And He said, "My Presence will go with you, and I will give you rest (Exodus 33:14).

This is what the Lord says: "The people who survive the sword will find favor in the wilderness; I will come to give rest to Israel" (Jeremiah 31:2 NIV).

In the second portion of Matthew 11, He says that *you will find rest for your souls*. According to the *Concise Dictionary of the Greek*,[5] the word *rest* here means *anapausis* or *resting place*. We need to seek this place of resting in Him, and when we seek it we will find it. It is a matter of choice. If we want to search for this place of refuge, we may. Additionally, it is a process of maturing in trust to the One we love. We grow every time we step toward the resting place.

Let me give you an example that has changed my life. In Song of Solomon 1 through 7, the Shulamite woman expressed her desire toward the beloved in different ways. Every verse is a stage where she found herself growing in her trust and love toward the Beloved as well as learning to dwell in His rest. If you have not studied this book, I recommend you do with the perspective that Jesus is the Bridegroom and believers are the bride. One of my favorite guides is by Mike Bickle.[6]

Here is the Shulamite's process of finding His rest:

1: *"For your love is better than wine"* (Song of Sol. 1:2).

She tests His love, but still doesn't embrace it. When I write about the Father's love here, I am speaking also about His rest. Love brings confidence about how we are in Him, and this knowledge brings rest.

2: *"I am my beloved's, and my beloved is mine"* (Song of Sol. 6:3).

Her heart is growing in love and rest. She can now say with confidence that she has found a place of resting.

3: *"I am my beloved's, and his desire is toward me"* (Song of Sol. 7:10).

At this stage in life, the Shulamite woman understood not only with her mind but with her heart that it is the Father's desire to have her dwell in His love and rest. It is a life-changing revelation. If you go deeper and study this process of growing in His love and searching for His rest, it will forever change you.

Rest is also a place of authority. It is a posture of trust. Why? Because it is in this place that our real identity is revealed to us. The identity of who we are in Christ. In that last verse the Shulamite woman had true conviction in her heart that she possessed everything that her Beloved (Jesus) had because she knew who she was with Him. As I surrendered my thoughts of fear, doubt, insecurity, hopelessness, and all sorts of negative feelings to God, He brought me peace and rest. It is a great exchange.

Between the tenth and eleventh chemotherapy doses, I had many ups and downs dealing with my health. Again, I exercised surrender and rested in my place of authority. I was done and ready to finish the chemotherapy cycle. Thus, we had family members in town, and as we entertained them such time together helped us shift our minds to other things. Although my body was weak, I had to learn to manage how to respond to different activities. At the same time, God expanded the revelation about knowing my place in Him in my heart every day. This was very deep for me. I could not have done it without the prayers of the saints from all over the world. People who didn't know me were praying for me. Prayers are the catalyst to bring heaven to earth. They were helping me to dwell in the secret place of His presence and rest. From there, I had to believe in His promises that He would take care of everything for me like He said He would in Psalms 127:1-2.

ONE MORE REASON TO THANK GOD

My mom's birthday was approaching. I really wanted to have an enjoyable day with her. She had left her home and busy life in Brazil behind to dedicate time to helping us in every way she could. Her sacrifice was precious to us and to God. We planned to honor her on her birthday by taking her to her favorite restaurant.

One week before her birthday, I had the tenth dose of chemo. After seventy-two hours, I spent the day at home, not feeling well at all. It was a rough day for me. During moments like those, when I was feeling weak, I decided to speak words of faith through Bible verses to my body, reminding myself of the promises that He has for me.

Let us hold fast the confession of our hope without wavering, for He who promised is faithful (Hebrews 10:23).

But if the Spirit of Him who raised Jesus from the dead dwells in you, He who raised Christ from the dead will also give life to your mortal bodies through His Spirit who dwells in you (Romans 8:11).

So Jesus answered and said to them, "Have faith in God. For assuredly, I say to you, whoever says to this mountain, 'Be removed and be cast into the sea,' and does not doubt in his heart, but believes that those things he says will be done, he will have whatever he says" (Mark 11:22-23).

This is actually a good exercise to practice in our everyday life. When we declare words of truth that come into alignment with the heavens, we are calling into existence something new. God created the earth by "speaking" out words that the elements of nature could not resist. He speaks and brings things into existence. That day I was doing the same. I was calling forth the promises and purposes of God for me and, at the same time, remembering in my mind who I was in Him. It was a great experience.

The following weekend I was ready to spend some quality time with Mom, rejoicing with her over the opportunity I had to be alive and well. One more time God demonstrated His goodness with priceless time like that. Our dear Father

God is detail-oriented. He loves to take care of small things for us, demonstrating His unfailing love.

ENDNOTES:

1. Johnson, B. (2009). *The Happy Intercessor.* Shippensburg: Destiny Image Publishers.
2. Striving. In *Merriam-Webster.com*. Retrieved on April 28, 2017, from https://www.merriam-webster.com/dictionary/striving

3. Surrender. In *Merriam-Webster.com*. Retrieved on April 28, 2017, from https://www.merriam-webster.com/dictionary/surrender

4. Zodhiates, S., Baker, W., Rake, T. & Kemp, D., (1996). *Hebrew-Greek Key Word Study Bible*, NIV. Chattanooga: AMG Publishers.

4. Kohlenberger III, J. R., & Swanson, J., (1996). *A Concise Dictionary of the Greek*. Chattanooga: AMG Publishers.

5. Bickle, M., Studies in the Song of Solomon, *MikeBickle*. Retrieved from http://mikebickle.org/resources/series/encountering-jesus-in-the-song-of-solomon

The Blood that Heals

Thirteen

THE BLOOD THAT HEALS

Dad was in charge of monitoring all my blood numbers. He put together a graphic with which we could see what was going on with my blood components since the beginning of the treatment. Every time I went to the hospital to take a dose of chemo, I had to do a blood test before the dose.

After the eleventh dose, my dad realized that my red cell numbers were lower than expected. We contacted the doctor to get his opinion. He decided to put me under a sequence of injections to stabilize this situation. I could not take them at home. I had to go to the hospital to take them. It meant one more day visiting the hospital. I am not a big fan of checking in as a patient. I prefer going to hospitals to comfort and pray for others, but since I started treatments I have felt differently. I have learned to be the person receiving help.

According to Dr. Eric Rosenberger, M.D.:

Red blood cells have several important roles to play in our bodies. The primary function of red blood cells is to carry oxygen from the lungs to the tissues around your body. As a secondary function, they are also a key player in getting waste carbon dioxide from your tissues to your lungs, where it can be breathed out. When red blood cells stop functioning properly, you can rest assured that many things are going to go wrong in your body.[1]

Let's start with the first function of the red cells—they bring *oxygen* to the lungs. Without oxygen, there is no life, so the red cells bring life to our body. This fact reminds me of the blood of Jesus shed on the cross, which brings us life when we accept Him as Lord and Savior.

Therefore, just as sin entered the world through one man, and death through sin, and in this way death came to all people, because all sinned (Romans 5:12 NIV).

Since we have now been justified by his blood, how much more shall we be saved from God's wrath through him! (Romans 5:9 NIV)

In him we have redemption through his blood, the forgiveness of sins, in accordance with the riches of God's grace (Ephesians 1:7 NIV).

The secondary function of the blood is to take out everything that harms our cells. The blood is responsible for cleansing us from all impurities. This is also a process of healing. If we accumulate things that contaminate our body, we will get sick easily.

Wash away all my iniquity and cleanse me from my sin (Psalms 51:2 NIV).

How much more, then, will the blood of Christ, who through the eternal Spirit offered himself unblemished to God, cleanse our consciences from acts that lead to death, so that we may serve the living God! (Hebrews 9:14 NIV)

In my case, I needed external help to support my red cells for them to function well. Otherwise, they were not bringing life to my body nor taking out all the undesired and harmful elements that were weakening my immune system. The injections were this help.

There are times in life when we need an "external help" to point the way, give support or encouragement, or extend a hand to lift up our hope so we can continue to run the race that we were called to run. Generally speaking, when our blood is healthy our body is healthy as well. So there is healing in the blood.

THE BROKEN BREAD FACTOR

From the beginning of the treatment, our spirits were awakening to the importance of taking Communion every day. My husband and I studied a lot about this and believed that we must not only take Communion in remembrance of Christ's death and resurrection but to declare that, through this act, health would come to my blood. We prayed the Word of God in Isaiah 53:

The chastisement [needful to obtain] peace and well-being for us was upon Him, and with the stripes [that wounded] Him we are healed and made whole (Isaiah 53:5b AMPC).

Broken bread also speaks about the brokenness of Jesus' body, dying in our place, in order for us to have life.

And he took bread, gave thanks and broke it, and gave it to them, saying, "This is My body which is given for you; do this in remembrance of Me" (Luke 22:19).

Jesus' body was given to us as a sacrifice on the cross for our redemption; we understand the vital importance of what He did. Praying and declaring the Word of God is equally important to bring health to our physical body. I would like to bring to your attention the matter of Communion. The origin of the word *communion* is the Latin word *communis* or *communio*. In English, it is the same word as *common* and late Middle English *communion*.

The corresponding term in Greek is κοινωνια (Koynonia), which is often translated as "fellowship".[2]

J. Henry Thayer's Greek Definitions expands the meaning:

1. Fellowship, association, community, communion, joint participation, intercourse.

2. The share which one has in anything, participation.

3. Intercourse, fellowship, intimacy.[3]

Communion it is not just the strong significance of the wine, symbolizing the blood, and the bread, the flesh of Jesus Christ. It is also a powerful act of *obedience* that binds us together in fellowship, intimacy, and participation with joyful and sincere hearts that brings revelation, clarity, and a sense of acceptance. We were created for *communion* with each other and with the Father.

We realized that in addition to healing, taking Communion:

1: Opened our eyes to see and acknowledge Him better:

When he was at the table with them, he took bread, gave thanks, broke it and began to give it to them. Then their eyes were opened and they recognized him, and he disappeared from their sight (Luke 24:30-31 NIV).

2: Opened the way for miracles to occur because we obeyed His Word and He is always with us:

When they landed, they saw a fire of burning coals there with fish on it, and some bread. Jesus said to them, "Bring some of the fish you have just caught." So Simon Peter climbed back into the boat and dragged the net ashore. It was full of large fish, 153, but even with so many the net was not torn. Jesus said to them, "Come and have breakfast." None of the disciples dared ask him, "Who are you?" They knew it was the Lord. Jesus came, took the bread and gave it to them, and did the same with the fish. This was now the third time Jesus appeared to his disciples after he was raised from the dead (John 21:9-14 NIV).

After Jesus went back to the Father, the disciples learned with Him to carry this practice, understanding the importance of it as He taught.

They devoted themselves to the apostles' teaching and to fellowship, to the breaking of bread and to prayer. Everyone was filled with awe at the many wonders and signs performed by the apostles. All the believers were together and had everything in common (Acts 2:42-44 NIV).

Every day they continued to meet together in the temple courts. They broke bread in their homes and ate together with glad and sincere hearts, praising God and enjoying the favor of all the people. And the Lord added to their number daily those who were being saved (Acts 2:46-47 NIV).

In both passages above, we can see that God brought increase and abundance among them. Miracles, signs and wonders, souls being saved, financial and many other blessings came that I think were not recorded here.

We realized that Communion was a powerful thing to do. It did not just bring to remembrance the death and resurrection of Christ but also our identity as sons and daughters, as it was in the beginning with man and the Trinity. A true love relationship between the Father and His children.

ENDNOTES:

1. Rosenberger, E., (n.d.). "The functions of red blood cells." *Actforlibraries.org*. Retrieved from http://www.actforlibraries.org/the-functions-of-red-blood-cells/
2. Communion (Christian). In *Dictionnaire Sensagent*. Retrieved on April 28, 2017, from http://dictionnaire.sensagent.leparisien.fr/Communion%20(Christianity)/en-en/
3. Koinonia. In *Bibletooks.org*. Retrieved on April 28, 2017, from http://www.bibletools.org/index.cfm/fuseaction/Lexicon.show/ID/G2842/koinonia.htm

Part 5
The End of the Journey

Fourteen

THE END OF CHEMOTHERAPY

Finally, the last day of chemo arrived. I had been counting down from day one and now it was a reality. I was extremely happy when I woke up that day. My husband gave me a card and flowers when I got home. I received my "diploma" when I left the hospital and all the nurses were cheering for me.

Even though I was happy, I was very weak. I couldn't believe that I didn't have to return to the hospital again. At that moment, I just wanted to rest and sleep. I received e-mails from family and some close friends. It was very encouraging.

The doctor gave me four weeks to rest before I started radiation. I had to go through the whole checkup process again during this period of time and the tests that would prepare me for radiation. He kept me busy.

One week later, our friend David Quinlan was in town as he had been at the beginning of the treatment. There was nothing better than coming together to worship Jesus with him. That was what we did, and the presence of God was sweet and enjoyable. We needed that during those days. God's manifest presence brings hope, perspective, purpose, joy, encouragement, and much more.

> *You make known to me the path of life; you will fill me with joy in your presence, with eternal pleasures at your right hand* (Psalms 16:11 NIV).

My spirit and soul were renewed in His manifest presence. It was a great blessing for us. After three weeks, we had the results of all tests, and because I passed on all counts we decided to spend the weekend close to the beach to break the routine a little bit. I was blessed to have this opportunity to enjoy the weekend, even with my limitations. One more time I saw God's goodness.

As soon as we got back, I visited the radiation doctor in order to do the simulation and adjusted all the details to begin the new treatment in a few days. I was not aware of what was coming.

STRENGTHENING YOUR DEFENSE SYSTEM

Chemotherapy drains your energy. You don't know where your energy goes. It is incredible and not at all pleasant. I wish there could be another treatment for diagnoses like mine. Chemotherapy is very aggressive, not only to the cancer cells but to the entire body.

One of the reasons I was feeling weak was because my immune system was being affected. It was fighting all the time to maintain my cells in healthy and perfect order. I know I mentioned this before, but it is an extremely important subject. The immune system is like an army that fights to maintain our body secure. It is our duty to help it with good diet, exercise, and plenty of rest. Sometimes we need an extra help from supplements. I found one that works for me and I took it during the treatments.[1]

The same way that this army inside of you is fighting on your behalf, there were dozens of people fighting in prayer for me. Those people, many of whom I never met, were raising up prayer for my healing to come to pass. Many of them were in the throne room every day, praying earnestly for me. My husband and I could feel when these prayers were intensifying.

Prayers connect heaven to earth. When we pray the Word of God, we agree with heaven. Listen well! There is power in agreement.

> *Again I say to you that if two of you agree on earth concerning anything that they ask, it will be done for them by My Father in heaven. For where two or three are gathered together in My name, I am there in the midst of them* (Matthew 18:19-20).

Prayers release angels to fight in our favor. I know I had angels fighting for me. Every day our prayers were not only for my healing but for those who were praying for me as well. We blessed them too. When we pray for somebody or something according to the will of God, we are blessed too. I knew that all these people who were praying for me were being blessed as we were.

I was taking supplements and vaccines to strengthen my immune system so my body could fight properly for my physical healing. In the same way, the army of prayer warriors God raised up was fighting for my healing. They played a very important role in our lives, and I am incredibly thankful for them. Even today, I meet people I didn't know were praying for me. God has His own methods to mobilize His people to His purposes and plans.

ENDNOTES:
1. In order to strengthen my immune system I took Immunocal. For more information, visit their website: www.immunotek.com.

Fifteen

THE LAST PART OF THE TREATMENT: MERCY

My treatment was almost done. I had a month of radiation to do. After a four-week break between treatments, it was time for the last part of this journey. Before I started, I had to do one section of simulation in order to map my body and mark all the points of reference to receive the radiation.

It was not easy for me to do the simulation session. In order to mark where the radiation shot was supposed to be, I had to use a mask molded only for me. This mask would help my head to be still and my chin to be far from the place that the radiation targeted.

After the mold was made, I had to test the mask. It was not easy for me to stay so tight to the table with my head in it. It was a feeling that I will never forget—uncomfortable and claustrophobic at the same time. I had never felt claustrophobia before, but I did now. It was a tough, panicky feeling that I had to deal with every day for the next month. What a challenge I had in front of me. I had to seek something new from God in order to have strength to go through that next phase of my journey.

There is always something new and fresh in God. He is an inexhaustible source of wisdom, peace, love, and so much more. We will never reach the end of His attributes.

Forget the former things; do not dwell on the past. See, I am doing a new thing! Now it springs up; do you not perceive it? I am making a way in the wilderness and streams in the wasteland (Isaiah 43:18-19 NIV).

Every time we seek Him, He comes. The radiation shots started every morning during those four weeks. Every day when I had to put on that mask, I asked the Lord to be with me; otherwise, I could not have stayed there. Even though I always had a family member accompany me during my sessions, I needed Him and His presence with me desperately. As I said above, God always has something new when we seek Him, so during that time He started to unfold His mercy to me.

First of all, God shows His mercy by reminding us that He is the Creator of all things. The deep revelation of our creator Father God brings us hope because He has the power to create a way where there appears to be no way.

"I am the Lord, your Holy One, Israel's Creator, your King." This is what the Lord says—he who made a way through the sea, a path through the mighty waters (Isaiah 43:15-16).

Many times, the first thing that comes to our mind when we speak about God's mercy is compassion. However, I have discovered that His mercy is not related only to compassion, but to other things as well. In Isaiah 54:10, the author describes two other meanings for mercy:

> *"For the mountains shall depart and the hills be removed, but My kindness shall not depart from you, nor shall My covenant of peace be removed," says the Lord, who has mercy on you* (Isaiah 54:10).

The first one is kindness. On my journey through this treatment, I saw the manifestation of His mercy though His kindness every single day. We didn't lack anything. God used people, circumstances, and many other things to provide for us. Many times during our prayer time, we felt like God was embracing us with the warmth of His presence. As a result, we started to pray or sing about the mystery of His kindness. It was one of those indescribable moments that I could not put in words, but I knew that something was changing from the inside of my heart and mind out.

Many times, I asked how His kindness could relate to difficult times like this. His answer for me at that time was His wrapping of His arms over me as a Father does with His children. At that moment, I just wanted to enjoy His love and forget everything else. I knew God was working on my soul and healing not just my body but my mind and emotions as well.

> *"With a little wrath I hid My face from you for a moment; but with everlasting kindness I will have mercy on you," says the Lord, your Redeemer* (Isaiah 54:8).

The second meaning is the covenant of peace. God makes an everlasting contract or oath with us that expresses one of His wonderful attributes—peace. Lexical Aids says of peace: *"it essentially denotes a satisfied condition, a state of peacefulness, a sense of well-being, both externally and internally."*[1] The Father's concern is not only with our spirit and soul but with our body too. He loves us as a whole. He is interested in my physical well-being, too.

He *"will be called Prince of Peace"* (Isa. 9:6) when His government will be established in the whole world. What is peace? In Philippians 4:7, Paul says, *"And the peace of God, which transcends all understanding, will guard your hearts and your minds in Christ Jesus"* (Phil. 4:7 NIV). His peace really transcends all understanding. It is like the wind—hard to explain, but you definitely can feel it.

I discovered that God likes to express His mercy through a covenant of peace with His people. He finds pleasure in doing that; it is a covenant that endures forever because His is a faithful God.

I will make a covenant of peace with them; it will be an everlasting covenant. I will establish them and increase their numbers, and I will put my sanctuary among them forever (Ezekiel 37:26 NIV)

During my last days of treatment, I realized that the expression of His mercy was deeper than I thought it was. It transformed and healed me as a whole—body, soul, and spirit. His mercy was a place of refuge in times of trouble.

Have mercy on me, my God, have mercy on me, for in you I take refuge. I will take refuge in the shadow of your wings until the disaster has passed (Psalms 57:1 NIV).

ENDNOTES:
1. Adams, L. (2011). "The point – Pursue peace." *Leah Adams.* Retrieved on April 28, 2017, from http://www.leahadams.org/the-point-pursue-peace/

Sixteen

FINAL MESSAGE

Dear friend, I encourage you to hide under His shadow of glory and goodness during the times of trouble. There you will find His mercy—that is, the manifestation of His everlasting loving kindness and the covenant of peace. His presence will give you strength through your journey.

My prayer is for you to keep your eyes on the Father's eyes. Don't look down, give in, or give up. He will guide your steps all the way. If you have never had a chance to surrender your entire being to the Father God or would like to reconnect with Him again, pray this prayer with me:

Father, I come to You surrendering my whole life to You today.

Forgive my sins and renew my mind. Heal me completely.

I know and acknowledge that Your blood <u>shed</u> on the cross was for me too, and it was not in vain.

I give You total access to my life. Open my eyes to see You in a different way that I never saw.

Jesus, reveal Your everlasting love and Your mercy to me.

Amen!

After I finished all the radiation shots, I was very happy to start to live a normal life with my husband, family, and friends again. This journey was not just mine; everyone who was close to me came through transformed too. We saw God.

It took me some years to have my level of energy back, but today I am totally healed by His love and mercy. A few years ago, I had the opportunity to participate in a triathlon race. It was a great experience for me.

I know the Father wants me to leave this message for you.

Be encouraged!

PRAYER FOR HEALING

Dear Father,

I believe in Your promises and in Your Word that says "by My stripes you are healed." I embrace these words. I declare that Your blood is not only over me, but is running in my veins and making me whole.

Thank You for Your sacrifice on the cross.

I am healed.

I believe and receive Your love.

Amen!

"The Spirit of God, who raised Jesus from the dead, lives in you. And just as God raised Christ Jesus from the dead, he will gaive life to your mortal bodies by this same Spirit living within you."
Romans 8:11

APPENDIX

LYRICS TO *"HEALING RAIN"* by Michael W. Smith

Healing rain is coming down,
It's coming nearer to this old town.
Rich and poor, weak and strong:
It's bringing mercy; it won't be long.

Healing rain is coming down,
It's coming closer to the lost and found.
Tears of joy and tears of shame
Are washed forever in Jesus' name.

Healing rain, it comes with fire,
So let it fall and take us higher.
Healing rain, I'm not afraid
To be washed in heaven's rain.

Lift your heads, let us return,
To the mercy seat where time began.
And in your eyes I see the pain;
Come soak this dry heart with healing rain.
And only You, the Son of Man
Can take a leper and let him stand.
So lift your hands, they can be held
By Someone greater, the great I AM.

Healing rain, it comes with fire,
So let it fall and take us higher.
Healing rain, I'm not afraid
To be washed in heaven's rain,
To be washed in heaven's rain.

Healing rain is falling down,
Healing rain is falling down.
I'm not afraid,
I'm not afraid.

ABOUT DIANA SCATES

Diana Scates is a creative strategist, intercessor, researcher, author, presenter, wife, and lover of God. She co-founded, with her husband, Rivers of Judah Ministries (RJM) and R. Well. RJM is an intercession and worship ministry dedicated to training and mentoring individuals who want to learn how to develop a lifestyle of intimacy with God. R. Well is a design company that adopted Design Thinking as a core discipline to identify solutions to problems in sectors like Architecture, Hospitality, and Healthcare. Diana has a desire to see the healing power of God touch people through prayers and worship, as well as technology channels. She lives with her husband, Lance, in Orlando, Florida.

Rivers of Judah Ministries

In 2002 my husband Lance Scates and I started prayer meetings (harp and bow style) every Friday night at Florida Christian University in Orlando, Florida. Since then, it has been a non-stop fervent worship and prayer every week. I never missed one meeting even though my treatment was on Friday mornings. The spontaneous music sung in those meetings lifted my spirit up and revigorated my body, soul, and spirit. I could even play the flute most of the time with Lance. Each Friday night meeting was an uplifting and refreshing moment for me.

I truly believe that music, when inspired by God, carries a healing power within it. I encourage you to visit Rivers of Judah Ministries (RJM) website playlist and listen to some glimpses of our meetings. Otherwise, if you are in Orlando area, you are more than welcome to visit us in our new location.

CONTACT INFORMATION

To contact the author to speak at your church, conference, hospitals, or clinics:

Diana Scates
Rivers of Judah Ministries
diana@riversofjudah.com
www.riversofjudah.com

To order books, listen to podcast, or raw spontaneous healing music visit www.riversofjudah.com.

www.ingramcontent.com/pod-product-compliance
Lightning Source LLC
LaVergne TN
LVHW051505070426
835507LV00022B/2931